BRIDPORT
& AROUND
THROUGH TIME
Steve Wallis

AMBERLEY PUBLISHING

First published 2014

Amberley Publishing
The Hill, Stroud, Gloucestershire, GL5 4EP
www.amberley-books.com

Copyright © Steve Wallis, 2014

The right of Steve Wallis to be identified as the Author
of this work has been asserted in accordance with the
Copyrights, Designs and Patents Act 1988.

ISBN 978 1 4456 3616 0 (print)
ISBN 978 1 4456 3644 3 (ebook)

British Library Cataloguing in Publication Data.
A catalogue record for this book is available from the
British Library.

Typesetting by Amberley Publishing.
Printed in Great Britain.

Introduction

Like other titles in the *Through Time* series, the photographs in this book are paired to allow the reader to compare old views, generally from the early decades of the twentieth century, with present-day ones. When making such comparisons, your first reaction is probably to see how things have changed. One of the points you may notice in this book, however, is that in many cases very little is actually different. In my view, this is a distinctive feature of Bridport and the surrounding area.

I have tried to match the viewpoints of my modern photographs as closely as I can to those used by the old photographers. In some cases, this has been impractical because the view from that location is now obscured by vegetation or new housing and the like, so I have had to find the closest place. I have also tried to keep to public rights of way.

My aim of taking photographs from as close as possible to the same spot as the original sometimes has had a 'warts and all' effect. My photographs sometimes show parked cars, street furniture, and so on; while not exactly photogenic, these objects are an essential part of modern life.

These photographs were taken during the spring of 2014, and when taking the coastal views the impact of the previous winter's storms was noticeable. Part of the coastal footpath at Burton Bradstock was closed, and elsewhere erosion was very noticeable. The latter has always been a fact of life for this part of the coast, but the storms and subsequent landslips had made people even more aware of it and its consequences.

Nevertheless, there are few if any better places to potter around in springtime than Bridport, West Bay and the surrounding villages, and I was pleasantly surprised by many of the locations and views I came across while hunting for the spots used by photographers from a century or so ago. The dates given are estimates of when the older pictures were taken.

The Town

View from Allington Hill, *c.* 1905 and *c.* 1940

The subject of this first chapter is Bridport itself, and to get an overview we will climb a couple of hills. We start on Allington Hill on the north-west side of the town centre, with three views taken at different times that show the development of the place. Both old photographs on the opposite page seem to have been taken in the same area where I took mine – the little park at the top of Park Road. In the foreground there is housing along the road called North Allington, partly obscured by nearer development in the modern photograph (*above*). The clock tower of the town hall can be made out left of centre, and the parish church in South Street is further to the right. A chimney and industrial area on the left of the oldest image (*opposite, above*) seem to have been demolished when the later picture (*opposite, below*) was taken. In the distance are Hyde Hill to the left, and North Hill to the right.

idport from Allington Hill

BRIDPORT FROM ALLINGTON HILL.

206562

BRIDPORT. GENERAL VIEW

Higher Up Allington Hill, *c.* 1910

Climbing further up Allington Hill we get a wider view across the town. The large building at the bottom of the hill, and in the lower-right section of these images, is St Swithun's church near the junction of West Allington and North Allington, and not far above it in the old picture we see a chimney in what is today St Michael's trading estate.

A More Southerly View, *c.* 1900

I think this attractive coloured view is also worth including here. Although it shows much of the same area as the previous two, it does extend a little further south, as you can see by comparing the position of the church tower. I have therefore paired it with a photograph of the southern end of the town from Hyde Hill, which includes the suburb of Skilling on the further hillside.

Looking From Hyde Hill, c. 1905

Next we go across to the east side of Bridport to look down on the town from Hyde Hill, with the aid of two old views that look across similar areas. From the old pictures in particular, we see the T-shape of the old town, with South Street running left to right across the middle distance, and West Street and East Street forming the bar of the letter to the right. A particular landmark is the tower of the parish church in South Street near the left-hand edge of the shot. Compare the modern picture, and development around the outskirts has blurred the T-shape somewhat, but it can still be made out. In the old views, the River Asker runs right to the left across the foreground, and beyond it is the railway line. Since then, Sea Road South, part of the Bridport bypass, has been built on the route of the closed railway, and development along it and Crock Lane can be seen in the foreground of my shot. Some of the field boundaries beyond can still be recognised, though. In the background, Allington Hill, where we stood before, is on the right (today almost surrounded by housing) and left of centre is the steep-sided Colmer's Hill, now with pines growing on the summit.

East Street, c. 1905

We drop down into the town for a tour of its three main streets, starting in East Street and looking in the direction of the central T-junction. East Street and West Street are thought to have been laid out in the thirteenth century as a planned expansion of the town. In this location, by the junction with Barrack Street, the Lord Nelson pub is on the left. It was originally called the 'The King Of Prussia', but Prussia became part of the unified Germany, so this 'unpatriotic' name was dropped at the start of the First World War. The pub was initially renamed 'The King of The Belgians' because he was on our side.

C. GEORGE, Pastrycook and :: Confectioner.

FANCY BREAD AND BISCUIT BAKER.

HOVIS, BERMALINE AND VIENNA BREAD FRESH DAILY.
—— Ices of all kinds. ———— Superior Mince Meat 10d. per lb. ————

Wedding Cakes a speciality. Rich Bride Cake always on hand or to order. Walker & Walton's British Wines.

Schools and Parties Supplied. Families waited on Daily. Muffins, Crumpets, etc.

George the Baker, c. 1905
Several doors along to the left of the previous view was the bakery of Charles George, at No. 42. The business had a long history on these premises, and George's Bakery only closed in 2013.

Street Scene, c. 1900

Our next viewpoint is outside what is now the United Reformed church. The Bull Hotel is the second building on the left. The old picture seems to show plenty of activity, but look closely and the people in the foreground are standing still and are generally facing the camera. To get so many people to pose, as well as keeping traffic out of sight, suggests a fair amount of organisation by the photographer, and probably the assistance of the local police in stopping that traffic.

The Town Hall, *c.* 1900

We move further along East Street. Some of the buildings on the left have been replaced, and the ground-floor shopfronts have changed, but otherwise the buildings are not that different. Here we get a closer view of the Town Hall and Market House, to give it its full title, built in 1785/86 on the site of a former chapel at the junction of South, West and East Streets. The distinctive clock tower was only added twenty years later.

**The Greyhound Hotel,
c. 1905**
We head on for this view of the Greyhound Hotel, which also shows some of the detail of the town hall. The hotel was built in the eighteenth century as a town house. Its frontage was then altered in the nineteenth century when it was converted into a hotel. The proprietor when the old image was taken was Walter Trump, who also advertised himself as an agent for the London & South West Railway. I assume this involved providing accommodation and perhaps onward transport for arriving passengers.

HANSFORD & SON,

4, EAST STREET, BRIDPORT.

Butcher's Shop, *c.* 1905
Part of the premises next door to the Greyhound Hotel is visible on the left side of the old picture on page 16. It belonged to Job Hansford & Son, who advertised themselves as butchers and farmers. Their shop is unrecognisable today.

health foods **HOLLAND & BARRETT** natural remedies

West Street, *c.* 1905

We move forwards a few yards to look from just inside East Street along West Street. My viewpoint is a little closer than the old one. There have clearly been changes on the right, on which I will expand later. The building furthest left is on the corner with South Street – it dates from the mid-nineteenth century and has features called *oeil-de-boeuf* (literally 'bull's-eye') at roof level. We will see its South Street frontage later.

HODDER'S
Commercial Hotel (Unlicensed).

Centrally situated.

Opposite the
Town Hall,

BRIDPORT.

Good :: ::
Accommodation.

Charges Moderate.
Private Entrance.

Hot and Cold
BATHS.

Bus to and from the
Station.

C. T. C.

Commercial Hotel, c. 1905
Now we look at a series of three adjacent businesses, which were the second, third and fourth buildings from the right in the last old view. This is the second one along, Hodder's Commercial Hotel, which boasted both hot and cold baths. This building survives, its frontage little changed on the first and second floors, opposite the town hall.

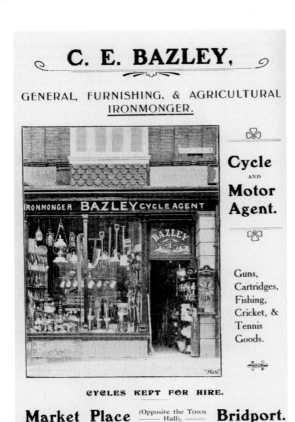

C. E. BAZLEY,

GENERAL, FURNISHING, & AGRICULTURAL IRONMONGER.

Cycle
AND
Motor Agent.

Guns,
Cartridges,
Fishing,
Cricket, &
Tennis
Goods.

"Maté"

CYCLES KEPT FOR HIRE.

Market Place (Opposite the Town Hall), **Bridport.**

Ironmonger's, c. 1905
Next door, at No. 1 East Street, were the premises of Charles Edward Bazley, an ironmonger and cycle agent. This property and the next have since been demolished. A job centre now stands on the site of Mr Bazley's establishment.

The Multitalented Mr Baker, *c.* 1905

Above is the larger shop of Thomas Brown Baker. He advertises himself with this picture as 'General Draper, Milliner, etc.', while in a contemporary trade directory he is described as a 'draper and insurance agent'.

THE ———— LEADING HOUSE

for all kinds of Plain & Fancy Stationery,

Books, Artists' Materials, Arms China, Devonshire Pottery.

SPECIAL SHOWROOM FOR FANCY GOODS.

LIBRARY IN CONNECTION WITH MUDIE'S. Subscriptions for short time.

The Largest Stock of **Local View POSTCARDS,** plain and coloured.

PRINTING :: :: IN UP-TO DATE STYLE, WITH DESPATCH.

Office of the " BRIDPORT NEWS."

ADDRESS

A Continuing Business, c. 1905
Part way along West Street on the left we find a business that has remained in existence for over a century. In 1903, W. & E. Frost, as the name was then, advertised themselves as publishers of the *Bridport News*, the *Dorset, Devon & Somerset Advertiser* and the *Bridport & West Bay Guide*. The only major changes to the frontage of this fine eighteenth-century building over the past century have been at ground-floor level. The three Doric columns are still there today, although their positions have moved.

West Allington, *c.* 1905

West Street extends to the end of the medieval town by the bridge over the River Brit. Its continuation is West Allington, which was the main road westwards before the construction of Bridport's bypass. From this vantage point a few hundred yards along and looking back towards town, we see some of the fine buildings constructed here in the early nineteenth century as the town expanded beyond its medieval limits. They are testament to the wealth of their owners, many of whom must have made their money in the rope industry.

GEORGE HOTEL,

Telephone **0186.**

Telegrams:— " Marshallsay, Bridport."

South Street, BRIDPORT.

Family & Commercial.

Fully Licensed.

POSTING IN ALL ITS BRANCHES.

Accommodation for Motors.

The George Hotel, c. 1905

We go back to the central crossroads and head down South Street. The second building opposite the town hall is the George Hotel, which, like the Greyhound round the corner, dates from the eighteenth century. The building to its right is the one on the corner of West Street, whose other frontage we saw earlier.

Looking Down South Street, *c.* 1905

The open area on the south side of the town hall has the wonderful name of Bucky-Doo Square, the origin of which has puzzled many a historian. Here we look from the square along South Street, with the tower of the parish church in the distance on the right and the projecting porch of the sixteenth-century building that today houses Bridport Museum on the left. Further to the left in the old picture, several of the buildings must have been demolished soon after the photograph was taken, since the large, brick building in their place today is early twentieth-century in style.

South Street

Bridport.

Reverse View, *c.* 1900

We head into South Street and turn around to look back at the town hall and Bucky-Doo Square. In this upper part of South Street, we are within what historians believe to be the oldest part of Bridport, dating back to Saxon times. Again, we see changes. On the left, the premises of Chesterton Humberts have filled in a gap in the old view, and across the street there are new buildings on the right side of the museum.

4860   *South Street, Bridport*

The Wide Street, *c.* 1900

Further down South Street we have this old photograph, which illustrates the parish church and its prominence within the townscape. It also shows us the width of South Street, which makes it an ideal location for a street market.

The parish church.

Bridport Parish Church.

The Parish Church, c. 1900 and c. 1905

Next we look at the parish church from a location a little further back up the street. The church is dedicated to St Mary. Most of the building dates to the late Middle Ages, although the chancel and side chapels at this eastern end were added around 1860. This work was undertaken by the architect John Hicks of Dorchester, to whom the young Thomas Hardy was apprenticed at this time. The pair of old views here provide a nice little study in foliage growth, probably over a period of about five years. The tree in the near angle of the building has grown considerably over this period, while some in the churchyard to the right seem to have been cut back or down. In the later image (below), trees have also been planted on this side of the road. My picture on the previous page shows the war memorial, erected after the First World War. There are eight panels on the wall behind that list the local men killed in that conflict. Since then, three more panels have been added with names of local people, including civilians presumably killed by bombing during the Second World War, and one dedicated to the single person killed in the Falklands.

The West End, c. 1905

Here we see the other side of the church. The yew tree by the near corner has certainly increased in girth, while the railings around one of the tombs have gone. In the modern image, this tomb appears as a low mound covered in foliage.

HERBERT N. HARRIS,

ENGINEER,

St. Michael's Foundry, BRIDPORT.

Motor Garage.   Inspection Pit.   Electric Light.

TRACTION ENGINE AND THRESHING MACHINE PROPRIETOR.

Estimates for all kinds of Heavy Haulage Work.

St Michael's Foundry, c. 1905
A little further back up South Street from the church, Foundry Lane leads off westwards towards the River Brit and the building that gave its name. The Edwardian owner was Herbert Nelson Harris, who advertised himself as a 'mechanical engineer, iron and brass founder, traction engine and threshing machine proprietor'. Although the foundry has long gone, the building on its site retains the name Foundry House.

The Surrounds

King Charles II Stone,
Lea Lane, Bridport.

E 34193

KING CHARLES II
ESCAPED CAPTURE THROUGH THIS LANE
SEP? XXIII. MDCLI.
WHEN MIDST YOUR FIERCEST FOES ON EVERY SIDE
FOR YOUR ESCAPE GOD DID A LANE PROVIDE.
(THOMAS FULLER'S WORTHIES)
ERECTED SEP? XXIII. MDCCCCI.

King Charles II Stone, c. 1905
In this chapter, we look at some features of 'wider' Bridport. Today, many of these locations might be considered suburban, but a century ago they were separate villages or in the countryside. Take the A35 east out of town in the direction of Dorchester, and you will find Lee Lane by the last houses on the left. On the corner, a memorial stone commemorates the escape of King Charles II through this lane when fleeing his Parliamentarian enemies after the Battle of Worcester in 1651. The stone was erected on 23 September 1901, and this old picture was taken soon after.

Hyde Road   Bridport

A Country Lane, c. 1910

It took me a while to work out where this old view was taken. It is entitled 'Hyde Road, Bridport', and while there is a place called Hyde not far to the south of the location of the previous view, no maps show a Hyde Road. After some searching on a pleasant morning, I realised the old photographer was in Walditch Road. In my view, you can just make out the junction with Crock Lane and Lower Walditch Lane in the background, not far from the A35. The path on the left is a shortcut to Crock Lane.

Hyde, c. 1905

We head east to Hyde itself, which is contiguous with the larger village of Walditch. The old view above looks across Hyde from the hillside to the east, with Bridport in the distance. The parish church is in the foreground, while further along the lane there is a large building constructed in the late nineteenth century as a court for the indoor game of real tennis. Beyond that, there is the large house called The Hyde, built in 1853 as the home of the Gundry family, who had long been prominent in Bridport's rope industry. My pictures below and overleaf show a closer view of the real tennis court, and a view of The Hyde, which is now a residential home, and its grounds from the hill to the south.

The Hyde and its grounds.

Bothenhampton, *c.* 1905

Bothenhampton lies on the south-east side of Bridport. It is effectively a suburb of Bridport now, though the old part of the village is still recognisable. The old picture, which was taken from the hillside across the little valley, illustrates the location of the village very well – it stretches along a lane on the hillside above a little tributary of the Brit. The modern photograph was taken from the top of North Hill, and illustrates the expansion of Bridport.

Bothenhampton Parish Church, *c.* 1900

Here is the new parish church, built at the western end of the old village in the late 1880s to the design of an architect called Edward Prior, some of whose other work we will encounter in West Bay. The church is prominent in the previous old and new views. The old church was at the opposite end of the village and was partially demolished when the replacement was built; the tower and chancel survive today.

Lovers Grove, *c.* 1900

This is one of two old images I have seen of 'Lovers Grove, Bridport', but I have been unable to locate it for certain. However, contemporary maps indicate that Coneygar Lane and other thoroughfares nearby are good candidates for this tree-lined route. Coneygar Lane is to the north-east of Bridport, separated from the centre by Coneygar Hill and running between the A3066 to Beaminster and the road to Pymore. My shot shows one of the best-preserved sections of 'old' Coneygar Lane.

Happy Island, *c.* **1900**

This scene is not far to the east of Coneygar Lane, on the River Asker, which flows into Bridport from the north-east. This little brick bridge, seen here from its eastern bank, is still much used by walkers on a path between the town's northern and eastern suburbs. In the background on the left of the old picture, there are signals on the old railway line into Bridport, which ran where Sea Road North is now.

HAPPY ISLAND, BRIDPORT.

Island View, *c.* **1910**

Here is another view of the same bridge. The viewpoint of the old picture (*inset*) seems to be a small island in the Asker just downstream from the bridge, which I suppose could be the origin of the 'Happy Island' name. I was feeling less intrepid than the Edwardian photographer, and stayed on the western bank.

Bradpole Parish Church, *c.* 1905

Bradpole lies further out on the north-east side of town. Although the urban area has stretched out to reach it, Bradpole still looks and feels like a village. Here is the parish church, which was built in the 1840s, with the spire being added in 1863. The church had a medieval predecessor, which was demolished to provide the materials for the present one, and this was located just inside the churchyard entrance.

West Bay

View from East Cliff, *c.* 1905 and *c.* 1935
Bridport had a harbour from medieval times, although its exact location is not known. It was abandoned after silting up, and in the early 1700s it was decided that a decent one was needed. The necessary Act of Parliament for its construction was granted in 1721, and twenty years later work was completed. As well as fishing, much of the activity centred on the export of rope and net products manufactured in Bridport itself. There was also a very successful local shipbuilding industry, and at one time in the early nineteenth century the shipyard on the west side of the harbour was England's second largest producer.

View From East Cliff

This place was once simply known as Bridport Harbour, but when the railway branch line that ran to Bridport from Maiden Newton was extended here in 1884, there seems to have been a major marketing campaign to make the place into a holiday resort. 'Bridport Harbour' probably sounded too work-a-day to contemporary ears, so the new station was called 'West Bay', and within a year or two the whole settlement has adopted the name. The Edwardian and 1930s views (*previous page*), as well as the modern photograph, taken on East Cliff, illustrate the expansion of West Bay from a relatively small settlement around the harbour. The distinctive large building is Pier Terrace. The harbour mouth was rebuilt in the early years of this century, and is now noticeably longer.

Pier Terrace, c. 1935
We begin a tour around the harbour on its western side, looking across at what is arguably West Bay's most iconic building, Pier Terrace. This is one of three buildings in West Bay designed by the architect Edward Prior (1852–1932), who worked in style of the Arts and Crafts Movement. It was built in 1884 and has gained the nickname 'Noah's Ark'. The seaward end was rebuilt after a fire in the 1930s, and the old photograph must have been taken soon afterwards. An extension has since been added on the other end.

Across the Harbour, c. 1935
We turn to the left through 45 degrees for this view across the harbour. The increase in the size and number of boats today is immediately obvious. Among the buildings opposite, the one on the left side with the pink walls is The Moorings, a later work of Prior's (built around 1905). The one with the white gable end is St John's parish church, built in 1936.

"GEORGE" Family and :: :: Commercial HOTEL,

TELEPHONE No. **4x.** ——— **WEST BAY.**

HEADQUARTERS:

West Dorset Golf Club.

Corinthian Sailing Club.

Bridport Swimming Club.

CATERING IN ALL BRANCHES.

Private Entrance. S. Boucher, *Proprietor.*

George Hotel, *c.* 1905

Set back from the harbour on the landward side we find the George Hotel. Presumably it was named after one of the first four King Georges, but the present building is a rebuild after a fire in 1839, nine years after King George IV's death. We see that an extension has been added on the right side of the frontage, and, in the middle section, what was once a door has become a window.

The North-East Corner, c. 1930
We continue our tour around the harbour at the north-east corner. Here our old view is impeded by a fine sailing ship, but it would be churlish to complain.

Querida, *c.* 1925

Round to the south-east corner of the harbour, we see another wide variety of vessels. On the far side (partly obscured by the larger vessel on the left of the old view) we see Querida, the third of Edward Prior's buildings in West Bay. To its left in the modern picture we see the new development on what was once the shipbuilding quarter.

THE CHAPEL ON THE BEACH. WEST BAY, BRIDPORT

The Chapel on the Beach, c. 1930

Set back from the south-east corner of the harbour, we find this fascinating building. It was built in 1849 as a Methodist church by a local shipbuilder, and it is rather telling that this denomination 'beat' the Church of England by nearly a century in constructing a place of worship in West Bay. Methodism was exceedingly popular among the working classes and those who wished to improve their social standing by hard work at the time.

The Pavilion, *c.* 1905
We go round to the harbour entrance, looking across to its western side. The old view shows a property called 'The Pavilion', which formerly stood there. The form of the building seems quite domestic, but its position suggests it has an additional function – perhaps it was used by the harbour master.

Rough Sea, West Bay, Bridport.

A Side View, *c.* 1925

Looking from a little further out along the harbour's eastern arm, the old postcard gives us a side view of the same building incidental to its main purpose of showing the rough sea. My photograph, taken on a much calmer day, includes the Salt House over across the harbour. This was a store for salt, which was then taken out by boats fishing off Newfoundland and used to preserve their catches. It became a museum and is now a community hall.

The Changing Harbour Entrance, c. 1900
Turning through 90 degrees to the left and stepping back (and, in the case of the old photographer, probably going upstairs in Pier Terrace), we achieve these comparative views of the harbour mouth. The curving wall in both shots seems to be the same, but the modern harbour entrance is clearly longer. The old version had no form of safety barrier along the water's edge, and there is an interesting wheeled crane on the further arm.

Sailing Ship, *c.* 1905

We go forward a little for this fine view of a sailing ship entering the harbour. In the old view, we see the same crane and the hut beside it. Other points to note are the projection on this side, on which a man is standing (there are none today) and the straightness of the harbour arms – today the western arm sweeps around to give greater protection from the prevailing winds.

The Harbour Mouth, *c.* 1920
Out on the western arm of the harbour we look across to the end of the eastern arm, with East Cliff beyond. The sea was rather less choppy when I took my picture.

Old River Mouth, *c. 1935*
From the harbour's eastern arm, we look across a very popular beach towards East Cliff. The beach is clearly higher today, a deliberate policy for sea defence. It is rather surprising to find out that the River Brit used to flow into the sea at this end of East Cliff. Its course was diverted when the harbour was constructed in the 1700s.

Gravel Extraction from Chesil Beach, *c.* 1920
We move closer to East Cliff and see a line of horses pulling a cart up the beach. They are part of an activity that would scare the life out of a coastal engineer today – quarrying gravel directly from the beach. The coming of the railway encouraged this, since the gravel could be loaded directly into freight trains for transport further afield. Even after the railway closed, gravel was sometimes taken away by lorry, and it wasn't until 1984 that extraction was stopped because of a realisation that loss of beach material would worsen flooding.

Digging in Progress, c. 1920
We now go even closer to East Cliff for a better view of this former local industry in progress. The two men are clearly digging a pit into the beach and shovelling the gravel into the cart while their horses wait patiently for what was probably a short trip to the railway station.

ESPLANADE, WEST BAY, NEAR BRIDPO[RT]

The Esplanade, *c.* 1930 and *c.* 1935
Next we travel around the harbour to the esplanade on the western side of West Bay for a view along the seafront and the coastline beyond. Changes include the removal of the groynes on the beach, the appearance of rock armour in the background and the spread of housing up the hillside of West Cliff. The esplanade has been divided by a road and a pedestrian walkway. We also glimpse some changes to the buildings behind the esplanade, but for a better view of these we need to head over to West Cliff.

THE PROMENADE, WEST BAY, NEAR BRIDPORT

The Esplanade from West Cliff, *c.* 1905 and *c.* 1920
Here are two images taken from similar locations partway up the path on West Cliff. They document not only the changes along the esplanade but also to West Cliff itself – the spur of land that is particularly prominent in the foreground of the earliest picture has long gone. The Edwardian picture shows a wider area than the others, and we see a lot of empty space on this side of the harbour, presumably the result of the decline in shipbuilding. There also seems to be very little development along the esplanade. The second image shows that chalets have now appeared in this area. There has been widespread redevelopment of the chalets since the 1920s.

West Bay, Bridport

The esplanade.

West Cliff, *c.* 1925

We climb almost to the top of West Cliff and look westwards along the coast. As my picture shows, erosion has also had a major impact, removing much of the land in the foreground of the old picture. The position of the old photographer near the cliff edge meant that Thorncombe Beacon (a couple of miles to the west beyond Eype) appears beyond West Cliff. Today, the change of angle from the retreating cliff edge means that only the distant coastline around Lyme Regis and into Devon appears in shot.

Symondsbury and Eype

Hidden Symondsbury, c. 1905
It is easy to forget that the quiet and extremely attractive village of Symondsbury lies little more than a mile from Bridport's town centre, as the crow flies at least. It is approached by narrow winding lanes, and if you come into the village on the one from the north, you might not be aware of Bridport at all. The old picture helps to explain why: Symondsbury lies in a natural bowl in hilly countryside. The picture also shows how close Bridport really is. The hill in the background is Allington Hill, our first viewpoint in this book, and the town is just beyond. The River Simene, one of the tributaries of the Brit, flows between village and hill.

Hidden Symondsbury, *c.* **1905**

The old viewpoint on the previous page was on Colmer's Hill, on the west side of the village, where there is no right of way today, so my photographs overleaf show two features in the village that can be picked out in the old image: the parish church of St John the Baptist and, to its right, the village school, which has a date stone from 1868. Both are built of local stone, the golden colour of which adds to the attractiveness of the village.

Symondsbury.

Duck Street, c. 1900

We move across to the other side of the village for a view back from Duck Street, where little seems to have changed over the past century. Perhaps the most obvious difference between the two images is on Colmer's Hill in the background. The pine trees that are such a landmark of the Bridport area today are missing from the old picture – they were not planted until the time of the First World War.

Eype Village, *c.* 1900

Eype lies towards the coast on the south-west side of Bridport, a little under 2 miles from the town centre. Its unusual name comes from the old English for a 'steep place', and the area is certainly hilly, especially along the coast. It is quite a dispersed village, and here we see the main settlement, sometimes known as Lower Eype. These views from the coast show the Victorian parish church on the skyline on the right (looking oddly faint in the old picture), which now doubles up as Eype Centre for the Arts.

Eype Cliffs.

Eype Mouth, c. 1910

The little road through the village, Mount Lane, makes its way to the coast at Eype Mouth. To the east the land rises into West Cliff, which we saw at West Bay, and on the west it ascends to Thorncombe Beacon. The viewpoints of the previous pair of photographs were on the coast path on the climb up to Thormcombe Beacon. Here we look from a little way up on the east to see lots of changes caused by erosion at Eype Mouth. The section of wall on the opposite side looks like a remnant of the one that curves uphill in the old view.

Looking From Higher Up, *c.* 1905
We climb higher on the same side for a good look across to
Thorncombe Beacon, with Lyme Regis visible on the coast
beyond in my picture. Erosion has also had an impact here
– the old viewpoint has gone, so I took my shot from the South
West Coast Path near the cliff edge and was some way north of
where the old photographer stood.

Chideock

View from Langdon Hill, *c.* 1930

Chideock lies 3 miles west of Bridport along the A35 coast road. As we can see here, the village lies in a bowl in hilly country. The viewpoint of both shots is Langdon Hill on the west side of the village. I think the old photographer was on the footpath that continues coastward from the entrance to the car park here, just as I was. The road from Bridport can be seen in the background, running through a dip between Quarry Hill on the left and Eype Down on the right.

Main Street, *c.* **1900 and** *c.* **1925**

We next look back towards the centre of the village from the eastern end. Chideock is very much a roadside settlement, with most of the houses extending along either side of the A35, which is called Main Street here. In the distance we see the parish church, while out of view on the north side of the village there is the site of a medieval castle, built here to control the strategic coast road presumably. The scene has not changed a great deal between the taking of the two pictures. The foliage in the gardens on the right is perhaps a bit thicker, but the same chimney is smoking in both views. Even today, the two buildings on the right have not changed much, although one has gained a thatched porch.

Chideock Village.

...OCK, BRIDPORT.

People in the Road, c. 1905

The old view looks very similar to the previous pair of views in Main Street. This is not surprising, since the viewpoint is only about one property closer to the village centre and many of the same buildings can be seen. What is surprising about this view is that the photographer has clearly posed a number of people, including children, in the road (one of the previous pair actually shows children sitting down and playing in the middle of the road). To anyone who has ever driven on this road, I need hardly say that you would be insane to try this today. My photographs may show few cars, but I did take them early on a Sunday morning.

Chideock House Hotel, *c.* 1925

We head along Main Street, crossing the bridge over the River Winniford and continuing a short distance, noticing that the road is getting gradually steeper. Turning back, we get this view, including the seventeenth-century Chideock House Hotel on the left. The colouring process used on the old image may not be entirely accurate, but it does look as though plaster has since been stripped from its walls to reveal the original stonework.

Cottages in Sea Lane, *c.* 1925
A few yards behind the previous viewpoint, Duck Lane leaves Main Street. It quickly divides into Sea Hill Lane and Mill Lane, both of which link to Seatown, though today there is a one-way system operating. Sea Hill Lane was once plain old Sea Lane, and here we find these rather attractive cottages, which were already over 200 years old when the first of these photographs was taken.

79. CHIDEOCK, SEATOWN – JUDGES LTD.

Seatown, *c.* 1935

Seatown is Chideock's equivalent of West Bay, albeit on a smaller scale and without the harbour. It lies about two thirds of a mile from the village at the mouth of the River Winniford. The viewpoint is on the South West Coast Path, and in the foreground we once again see evidence of erosion. We look down to Seatown, where the Anchor Inn is prominent in the view, and beyond to the limestone of Golden Cap, the highest cliff on England's south coast.

Burton Bradstock

The Village, c. 1930

In this last chapter, we go back to the other side of Bridport. Burton Bradstock lies about 3 miles south-east of the town, on the coast road to Abbotsbury and Weymouth. Its attractive old centre and the proximity to the coast make it very popular with visitors. Here we look from the hill to the south-west, from where the modern view illustrates the village's expansion up the further hillside. Shipton Hill is visible on the skyline to the left.

Shadrach, c. 1925

We start a short tour of Burton Bradstock and its beach over on the north side of the village. Here we look northwards along Shipton Lane at the start of its journey over to Shipton Gorge. The viewpoint is a little green at the junction with Shadrack Lane (back to our left in this view) and Middle Street (back to the right). The area in front of us is called 'Shadrach' on old maps. The present houses on the right must have been built around the mid-twentieth century.

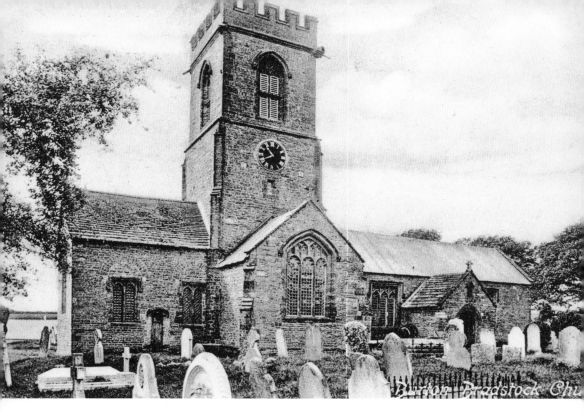

Parish Church, *c.* 1900

Going down Middle Street, we reach the late-medieval parish church. Looking at the present-day view, we see that, in common with many other churchyards, the gravestones have been removed. The stone tombs were left in place, as was the cross on the right.

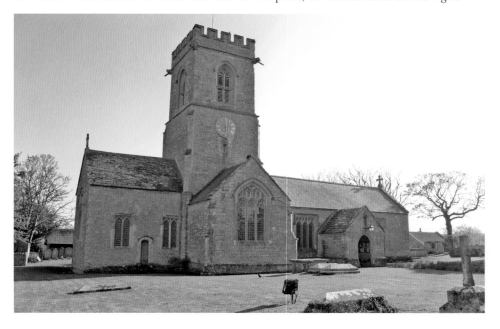

High Street, *c.* 1935

We move westward into the village's High Street. The old view shows a pub sign, and from the symbols it becomes clear that this is for the Three Horseshoes Inn, which is just out of shot to the right. There is also a rather nice phone box nearby. The modern view includes a sign for the village post office, again over to the right.

Crossroads, c. 1905

Going back south down the High Street, we cross the bridge over the River Bride and reach a road junction. The High Street bends round to the east, changing its name to Common Lane, and continues towards Abbotsbury. I think the old photographer went into the garden of a property on the corner of the two other routes at this junction: Southover and Cliff Road. Mine was taken at road level and includes part of the modern garage.

Burton Bradstock.

View From a Footpath, *c.* 1910

Just into Cliff Road, a footpath branches off to the east and gives us this vantage point. The top of the garage is in the lower part of my photograph. The house across the road looks quite new in that picture, but compare with the old and you see it there too – it is just that some of its features have been modernised.

Hive Beach, c. 1930

As its name suggests, Cliff Road heads south to the coastline. Formerly, you could then follow it for a short distance east to Hive Beach and the viewpoint from which the old photograph was taken, but this section has been closed because of erosion. Nevertheless, Hive Beach can still be reached easily, by car down Beach Road to the east, for example. My photograph was taken from a lower level because of the closure, but you can still see the extent of erosion on the far hillside, particularly by comparing the location of the large hut in relation to the cliff edge.

BURTON BRADSTOCK BEACH NEAR BRIDPORT.

Burton Beach, Bradstock

Valentine's Series

31106

Coastal Erosion, *c.* 1900 and *c.* 1930

We move over to the other cliff and look back for this sequence of pictures that again illustrates coastal erosion in action. The cliff's edge has moved progressively closer to the two Victorian seaside villas (which were originally called 'Burton Villas'). Also, the second photograph indicates that the location on the cliff from where the earlier picture was taken has since been lost, and the modern photograph (*overleaf*) illustrates the continuing erosion rather graphically.

Burton Beach, Bradstock, today.

THE CLIFFS, BURTON BRADSTOCK.

The Cliffs, c. 1930

Finally, we go down onto the beach for a closer look at the cliffs. We can safely assume that the people who chose this location for their tent had very little awareness of coastal erosion and rockfalls.

The Jurassic Coast

Paul Harris

This unique selection of images, accompanied by an insightful commentary, is the perfect companion for anyone who loves this beautiful stretch of coastline.

978 1 4456 1917 0

96 pages, full colour

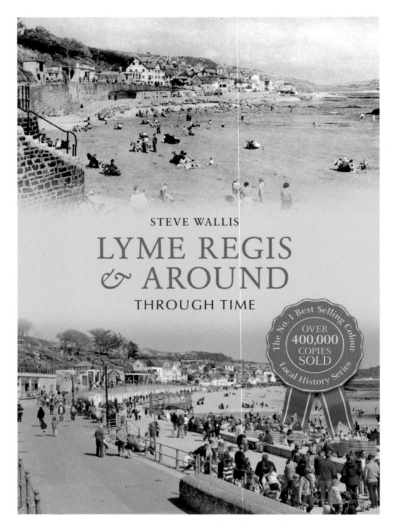